ETERNAL ARTIST

EMILY B
SCIALOM

Acknowledgments

Thank you to my family and friends who've stuck by me and provided a loving environment in which I can flourish.

My sincerest gratitude to William Hartston for his encouragement, inspiration and literary expertise.

My heartfelt thanks to Michael Lumsden for designing the cover of this publication and generally being a stalwart I can rely upon.

Thanks to Carraig Dillon for the long conversations filled with priceless insights, seeing the reward in rebellion and the hope in art.

Many thanks, too, to all those who contributed to or permitted me to quote them for this book.

Index

Introduction

I began writing this book in late May 2019 and finished in October 2020. It has emerged as 500 lines of poetry and observations from all realms of my life.

I originally planned to have them in chronological order. However, after discussions with various friends and family members I decided to take their advice and organise the collection of scribbles into categories, which you will soon read as the final piece of literature you have in your hands.

The lines are sometimes overheard, quoted or channelled, but mostly they are original thoughts I have had about my life. Every line, I feel, contributes something to the poetic feast you see before you.

During the past year there have been many changes to my day-to-day existence. I used to go to London to see friends and maybe take the odd trip to Brighton or Eastbourne to promote my first two books, 'The Religion Of Self-Enlightenment' and 'The Rivers'.

Since the Covid-19 pandemic emerged early this year 'Eternal Artist' has gone from being an outgoing and occasionally buoyant piece to a more contemplative, globally questioning creation.

During the making of the book I went through two breakups and lost a handful of close friends to either

Covid-19 (Rufus Fox) or mental health issues. This goes some way to explaining why there are so many mixed emotions displayed in the finished version of 'Eternal Artist'.

I have edited a few passages out of the book in order to keep it moving forward and prevent it from being burdened by lengthy prose. Obviously, you may want explanations for some of the lines, but in leaving them partially shrouded in mystery I hope they will be rendered relatable.

I hope this goes some way to explaining how the novel was created. I know some of you will have come here as a result of my Twitter account, which I have used to share every line of this book as it was formed. Thank you for coming with me on this journey and I hope you will all enjoy the finished piece.

Emily B. Scialom
22 October 2020

1. Nature

Raindrops like kisses from Heaven.

When we hear Neil Young play the music rolls over us like waves going onwards into an infinity we will never live to see.

The world needed that!

Her life was relatively short to have gone so crushingly wrong.

A story as ancient as time itself.

I touched the sun and I survived.

Black holes in his eyes.

You've got to learn to embrace death: everyone you know is going to die, as are you.

Beautiful, powerful, carefree women!

Something to submerse yourself in.

It really makes me reflect on the ephemeral nature of life.

It's weird life, isn't it? One minute you're the kid walking back from school, the next you're the adult walking past the kids walking back from school.

10

The trouble is we are all divided by gender, skin colour and ethnicity. If we could work together for the greater good we would be much stronger. One love, brothers and sisters. If we can pull through this we can pull through anything. Two World Wars and one climate catastrophe!

Destroying those weaker than yourself does not make you stronger, only crueller.

Another scar on the journey of life.

I always think of the world as a wayward teenager. Hopefully our adulthood will be more peaceful.

It's a merciless destruction of everything except for white men.

And it's really quite a scary world when you realise there are people like that out there.

The better it is, the more divisive it becomes.

No one wakes up a butterfly.

If I die now, I die happy.

So many disasters.

We're like ants trying to understand the sunrise.

Some people are bastards, you're bound to encounter one or two of them.

Up or down? Future or past?

Eternal artist.

Whatcha doing? Just watching the rain.

A tragedy beyond all measure.

An island of calm.

The sea of the night laps against my window.

Everything's okay apart from the world is falling apart.

The human experiment has gone wrong.

The triumph of nature.

Can't post the truth.

It's an avoidance of death; it's not life.

I am of the air yet I can barely breathe.

A sentence can change your life if you read it in a certain way, in a certain light.

My smile feels rusty.

The philosopher's going to philosophise as sure as the chef's going to cook.

It's dawn on the edge of the world.

The body forgives your misdemeanours, the Earth provides.

All very human.

An absence of anything.

A teardrop took me by surprise.

It's a festival of the weird.

A black hole of principles.

One by one our heroes fall.

Drop a rock of truth in the pool of life and watch the ripples go.

Your power is growing.

Mining for literary diamonds.

I write because I'm in pain.

It's survival of the greediest.

A moment of stillness.

Dwarfed by nature.

The sweetness of strangers.

Sail the seven seas of creativity.

That's the thing with art: everyone sees something different.

I'm in full bloom.

I suffer.

But compared with refugees we don't suffer and that is just reality.

Comparisons are odious.

The whole world is on a knife edge.

If the world were a person, he or she would be holding a loaded gun to their head and thinking about pulling the trigger.

A deathbed classic.

Fuelled by silence.

Eerie-eyed.

The destruction of nature before our very eyes.

That's humanity in a nutshell: completely barmy but utterly brilliant.

A world without judgement would be a beautiful thing.

Good at life.

Pain is the artist's treasure.

A day that promised little and delivered less.

Smoking in graveyards.

There's enough sorrow in the world.

Life's a killer.

Nothing's ever perfect.

2. The Mind

I feel horrifyingly sane right now because I'm free of all the things that make me mad.

And don't think I don't know my flaws because I know them all too well.

"It's like all my thoughts in a row."

"Well, all of your thoughts are important, Emily."

An injection of intelligence.

Victimised by vanity.

Watching people slowly lose their minds.

All the chaos of a daydream.

I like calm.

Assigning understanding where there is none.

Happiness comes in waves, it'll find you again.

I wish I had just a little bit more money or a little less ambition.

Educated few against the uneducated many.

The first casualty of alcoholism is the truth.

We have the freedom to be whatever we want to be, and that means the freedom to choose to be incarcerated.

Shyness has been one of the greatest enemies of my life.

I've SEEN the edge, and it is a nasty, cruel place.

Conscious elevation.

As long as you can speak your truth life can be bearable. It's when you can't speak your truth that they've finally driven you insane.

Future minds.

I can't understand the way a lot of people see the world - in tearing each other down like we do, we tear down ourselves.

It's just the truth, don't pay it any mind.

I've had two good ideas today, which is more than most people have in their lifetimes.

Caring about the world is a dangerous venture.

Bad dreams, feeling of ominousness.

Don't fall off the wagon of normality.

Everyone seems insane when you only hear half their conversation.

You're allowed to have a failure of imagination sometimes.

Everyone's a c*nt and you know you ain't.

A really bad dream.

Feeling down like there are no good people in the world.

I'm understood by someone, that's a victory for the day.

These are the things I think about.

Can only the mad touch the stars?

I love your conclusions, even if I don't concur.

The day vs Emily.

You forget who you are.

Sometimes I just sit there remembering.

Learn to be honest.

Damaged children.

Know your heart.

Obsession with a moment.

A dreamer's mind.

Bit of a nightmare, but we made it to morning.

A pain that no one else knows about.

I'm connected to things I don't understand.

The exchanging of masks.

Forgotten promises.

Identity crises, the teething pains of evolution.

I take refuge in words.

Think about life, not death.

Breaking waves of creativity.

Ignorance is the canvas upon which you paint.

Daydream more.

Imagine if the world made sense.

It's like living in a psychiatric hospital.

Why am I so unbearable?

We're in a place of not knowing.

How do you stay sane in an insane world, when there are no barometers except for what's within?

I'm at maximum sorrow.

Please accept my admiration.

Superb effort at normality.

You know the kind of torture that caused Van Gogh to chop his ear off? Yeah, that.

Tell me all your secrets.

A truly amazing secret.

You forget who I am.

We're processing unspoken wrongs.

A noble aim.

Sanity has its own burdens.

If you weren't worried about the world you'd be crazy.

Sanity's underrated.

I'll do whatever it takes to be happy.

Are you frightened of sadness?

I'm suicidal on a good day.

There's probably not much time left to pursue your dreams.

The songs that no one knows.

To feel excitement about the future in this day and age is quite the feat.

I'm terrified of what I deserve.

Unexpressed thoughts.

Limited edition knowledge.

A right-headed person.

Madness is the new norm.

I would never burn any art except CDs with misogynistic lyrics.

You don't realise how young you are.

This is the dream.

We all make our own worlds.

You got in the way of my dreams.

It's a dangerous game dangling someone's dreams in front of them.

Trying to live other people's lives.

Here's to those who fought unknown battles to their unvisited graves.

3. Friends

Emily and Justin in Cambridge streets, going to see their friend Rufus in slow motion.

None of us has any hope, but we're all in this together, and there's a beauty in that.

They're too self-absorbed.

She can't be on time for love nor money.

He could teach me so much.

Fluffy af on the train to Londinium.

Thank you for keeping the flame alive.

He's like a boxer who's just lost a fight.

She's writing a book - she's gonna do one on us!

Onwards to an awesome future, friend.

I feel like everything he does is profound and he doesn't even know it.

Keep on fighting, brother.

Well done, Andy, it seems like he was really on the edge.

Listening to Zappa round a friend of mine. Give us a

call if you're so inclined.

The opposite of thieves.

Relentlessly jolly.

If I had anything to throw up I would have thrown up already.

At last! Someone to be excited by.

Never your Yes Man.

Like an unpaid nurse.

Not an idiot!

I've known him for years and I don't know the first thing about him.

Rufus was a diamond on a beach.

In my cult you are my favourite student.

You make me want to live.

It grows dark, and his is the hand that cups the candle.

I just got called "the Egyptian Queen of Peace" - and I can deal with that.

"I haven't been angry for some time."

"Neither have I!"

"It's almost like we're peaceful now or something!"

Only the darkness is your friend.

She's an angel with distorted colours.

Smoking in victory.

Fake friends are no friends.

I'm a picture of serenity without you.

I have a story and a secret with your name on it.

I'm happy without you.

4. Family

"Artists aren't meant to be rulers, they're meant to be outsiders," Dad says.

"Charlie knows how to keep focused and live in the present moment."

"Yeah, it's just the present moment can't be too pleasant for him now."

"Well, that's all we've got, Em."

"Lilly's just too cute. It hurts me. I mean, what are we going to do with her?"

"Love her forever!"

"Worship her like a Goddess!"

"No one ever has autonomy over your authenticity," Dad says.

She's wobbling her way to freedom.

Sporadic beady eyes.

Every day she does something to be proud of.

The grand hall of your life has just been entered.

That child is wildly awake.

I wouldn't change today even if I could.

She's drunk on love!

A linguistic growth spurt.

Is there anything purer than a child eating rain?

"I will write a letter to the milkman in a rinsed bottle
/ Redemption is as you find it when you're alone,"
Mum sung.

"Strong roots form from past flowers." Aggie
Andrews

5. Quotes

"We forget our own minds are the riddle, and we desire to forget to solve it." Sudeep Bhalsod

"I'm none of that. I'm a dog, the woo. That's it. An artist." Pop Smoke

"Until the song that is yours alone to sing falls into your open cupped hands." Martha Postlethwaite

"I'd much rather confuse myself with something more beautiful." Carraig Dillon

"Psychedelic sonic creation." Joe Taysom

"Unapologetically searching." Beth Ransom

"The sadness will last forever." Vincent Van Gogh

"Broken home, broken hearted." Canibus

"Miss getting lost." Sonia Puri

"Like a squeak in the cacophony. Diamonds trodden underfoot, unnoticed in the mire." Johnny Superstrings

"Reputation is your religion." Rumi

"Life lies, a slow suicide." Richie Edwards

"If you have faith, you know you are loved." Philip

Anderson

"The spirit indeed is willing, but the flesh is weak."
Jesus

"They will be destroyed," the religious say with
smiling faces.

"My soul's an oasis,
Higher than the Sun." Bobby Gillespie

"Beauty is God's handwriting." Charles Kingsley

"Each of us is immortal." Dr Brian Weiss

"The act of creation is disruptive." Bruce Marinello

"Start a revolution." Citizen Eco Drive

"Yesterday was today once before." @TheClearCider

"Sometimes you have to invent the thing you're
looking for." Jeff O'le

"If you expect anything, expect to be disappointed."
GrooveSun

"There are moments in life where you learn nothing.
These are the moments you are here to teach."
Patricia Sund

"Note to self and others: self-care is not narcissism."
Keilah Kay Folkertsma

"Isolation isn't a particular curse, it's just where good
people tend to end up." Unknown

"When I talk, it's not a rant. It is a symphony of
ideas." Kanye West

6. Poetry

The authenticity of the poetic flame.

Writing eternalises the present moment.

People have forgotten poetry in the modern world.

Rumi sails as close to God as anyone in my eyes.

Good words should be savoured.

Sin

Four over, one is screaming

Promised I wouldn't get this drunk again

Naked again, no bin

Every little thought that I think is a sin

We Are Love

I love you 'til my mind aches

I'll love you 'til my heart breaks and all souls are one

You hurt me more than words could ever tell

You loved me less than death or sadness

I'm yours now

As I was yours before

I'll be yours forever

My education destroyed my mind

My purpose of life corrodes my worth

My religion offends my soul

My government just destroys my world

The sun will make you blind

The dark will make you blind

Fear will make you blind

But when I close my eyes

I find we are love

Strong

Life is difficult

The road is long

Keep your head up

And try to stay strong

Friendship

My window is a portal and I am holding on tight.

Your love is a candle

I am the night

I wrap around you like a friend

I Love You, Too

There is no time like the present

Ultraviolets are blue

Have you ever thought that I love you like you love
me too?

Perfection is right in the centre of your eyes

Goddamn this feeling

I Don't Wanna Talk About Jesus

Don't wanna talk about Jesus

Don't wanna talk about the wars in foreign lands

Don't wanna talk about the homeless on the streets

Don't wanna talk about the cruelty of the beat

War

The war rages on

No time to drop your spear

Your rock, your axe, your gun

Your big red flashing button

All must be kept close

For harm must be inflicted to stay well

Both sides say this, though

And the confusion becomes absolute

Believe

Believe in a better tomorrow

Believe one day there will be rain to quench the arid
landscape of your faith

Believe that one day black, white, yellow, red skins
will walk together under the forgiving sun

And all this will be past

With a future as golden as a polished crown

Sitting on the head of The One

7. Romance

Men are as treacherous as the day is long. And they will still be treacherous tomorrow.

"It's like the gates of Heaven."

"It is with you beside me," he said.

A walking love song.

"If Love Is The Drug Then I Wanna OD. I mean, is there a better song title than that?"

"Yeah, but that's the worst, though: it's when the medicine becomes the poison."

Dreaming of you.

Never mess with a broken-hearted person.

I'm heartbroken for him.

Please stop crying.

Did I get used to the sadness?

My heart was broken before we even began.

She is a thing of real beauty.

You are the star to my Sun and we are one.

Satisfaction. Always just beyond our reach.

It's like burning my heart.

I had everything but love.

We're all just trying to be loved.

Love in writing.

He's got a blind spot the size of Jupiter when it comes to women.

Always be yourself. The right people will love you.

It's hard to see the beauty of life when you're going through a break up.

Described by a medium as "a heartless narcissist surrounded by dark energy"

No one on my mind.

A song for the sadness.

Thank you for the love.

Meant to be.

You know who I am.

We made some awful memories.

It could have been so different.

Make me want to be here.

Please read 'The Beautiful And Damned' by F. Scott Fitzgerald.

I thought you'd fallen in love yesterday.

I can't control my charms.

I'm having a fantasy with you.

Where do I sign for your heart?

Glad the universe showed me your true colours sooner rather than later.

I've learnt intimately the depths of a narcissist's heartlessness.

I'd rather someone said "I hate you" than "I love you" and stab you in the back.

People of the past torment my mind, people of the future I have yet to find.

We're all afraid, in our own way, of real intimacy.

You see me as I am.

Even the good can hurt.

The ego of a Roman Emperor.

You can haunt without having died.

8. Politics

She pondered for a minute the death and destruction of the D-Day landings: the heroes we've lost, the heroes we've gained.

If the children don't care about their futures, nobody will.

"Get out of my adopted country!"

I refuse to participate in my own destruction.

"He's not Jewish so he's an infidel to his wife."

"Yeah, he's an infidel to me, the f*cking c*nt!" Dad said about Netanyahu.

Trump is a raincloud above all our heads.

The wrong are seldom lonely.

So long as the music's loud enough you can't hear the world falling apart.

It's the exploitation of people with talent by people with no talent.

It's as shocking as the idea of a better future.

This is what it feels like to be complicit in our own captivity.

Basically genocide before the eyes of the world.

Jerusalem's the spiritual beating heart of the world and there's always been blood on its streets. I mean, what does that say about us?

The law is not a moral barometer.

In this world of greed it may take a few comets from the working classes to bring messages of their struggles to the masses.

Oh, I am so shocked to my core that a Tory has taken a shot at disabled people.

F*ck politics. Stay alive. You can do this.

I'm saner than anyone who votes for Trump.

Evil people standing in the full glare of the light.

I don't care about Brexit anymore. You've finally broken me. Give me a tie-dyed passport with a free acid tab. I want borders up my arse. I want avocados for no less than £100 and insulin only for those with a desire to stay alive anyway. Everyone else can go f*ck themselves.

You'd be lying if you weren't lying!

Control the world.

Do you only have evil heroes?

Dark entertainment.

We are speaking words that must be said: Black
Lives Matter!

Straight chilling until the world improves.

Stuck on this island of racists and fools.

They've bought themselves out of justice.

Someone has to be right.

9. You've Gotta Have A Laugh!

"Modern music is like icing, but on top of poo."

You're only eccentric if you're rich; if you're poor you're mad!

You're like drunk Google!

It smells like someone can't wash their own arsehole around here. Hope it's not me.
F*ck you all and your bad taste.

At least you've still got your humour, my lovely. When life claims that you know you've got a problem!

Never has a truer word been spoken than to call that man a c*nt.

I see jokes in everything.

People think I'm good for nothing because I've got nothing to do.

It's better to be unconscious than to be wreaking havoc.

Best case scenario? We're all f*cked.

Banal mongs.

Apocalypse porn.

When I was on my walk, wearing a cape and surgical mask, someone shouted "YOU LOOK LIKE A SUPERHERO!!" across the car park at me. I am fully aware the only superheroes around here are the NHS workers.

"Things will be better in the future."
"Fingers crossed."
"Sanitised fingers!"

I know why we attract bad men. We're human emotional hospitals!

Hold your horses before you blow all your candles out.

Is there any way you could reduce the fee for poor folk like me?

You are not an educated person. Give up the art of conversation.

Mother Earth has been arrested.

Up a cul-de-sac without a paddle.

Having explored the outer reaches of the schedule, I can confirm: there isn't always something to do.

10. Faith

"My faith is stronger than theirs in some ways because I'm looking for God in all religions, not just one. I'm looking for God in Hinduism, I'm looking for God in Buddhism, I'm looking for God in atheism, I'm looking for God in everything."

"But haven't you found God in all of them? There's God in all of them."

I know the answer.

I am a pioneer.

Peaceful as hell.

Daring to exist.

It's a bit like a soul bath, isn't it?

A search for peace.

I'm seeking the truth, not applause.

Each time we fall down in pieces we rebuild ourselves.

If you're not making the world a better place you're wasting your time.

Shot down by angels.

Spiritual refugees.

Even your shame is sacred.

How far I've come.

You don't have to cry about life all the time.

A scream trapped inside my soul.

It's not an easy ride, even if you're a dickhead.

A Christian heart.

Yeah, it's a tough old world trying to be holy in a very mortal realm.

I cling to truth like a life raft.

I can't wait for the future.

Be thankful to watch others fly, even if you yourself are stationary.

We will all kiss the sky one day.

I've got a feeling I will get to Heaven and God will say, in a sarcastic voice, "Well, that went well!"

The character of the soul.

Heaven surrounds you.

I was an asshole, now I'm a soul.

Basically, it's wicked.

And it's sad, y'know, because you want to be in the realm of light and spirit but in the material world you can only glimpse it.

Is this acceptable?

It's nice to be believed in.

It's nice to believe in you.

Give it credence.

Ancient souls.

I'm trying to be a Saint, but I'm just another sinner.

Which I was,

Which you are,

Which I am.

I am blind, acting as though I see.

I don't understand the mechanics of religion.

The power of truth.

Unconditional self-love.

Keep God in mind.

A graceful trip into history.

Man-God.

I'm willing to be embarrassed in order to speak the truth.

Schynheiligheid (fake holiness)

The Gods wouldn't be so generous!

90% uncertain what tomorrow will bring.

It's like a collective self-reflection.

A complicated blessing.

Knock and Heaven will answer.

The only real victory is being true to yourself.

I am naked before God.

Hang hope.

My dreams are God's dreams.

You couldn't have faith in me?

Carve your future like your words.

Heavy prayers.

The voices of the dead fill the air.

A leaning towards love.

Each one of us has blessings we can't describe.

I've got everything to live for.

To mark a remarkable life.

That makes my soul's heart sing.

Why is truth so uncomfortable?

The meditators are taking over.

A vacation of souls.

A spiritual mountain.

My physical body might be white and female, but my
soul is many things.

This is my progress.

Grace grew.

I picture God waiting patiently for me.

Of all the fates the Gods could bestow.

I love You faithfully.

You're my guiding light.

I believe they call it "healing".

The changing of deities like the changing of clothes.

You give me the strength to go on.

You remind me of God.

Love the lost souls.

A reason to wake up.

Enlightenment or death: which will come first?

Ropes sawn.

Interacting with the gods.

Kindness was repaid.

If you want to know the truth about something who do you ask?

God is so much more than the faiths He/She breeds.

God is beautiful.

A sacred secret.

A shining light to guide you right.

Power, money, fame: a myriad of mistaken deities.

I'm pretty much there.

Can you do better?